WILDLIFE VIEWING AREAS

Iowa Ecoregions

- ☐ Central Irregular Plains
- ☐ Driftless Area
- ■ Interior River Valleys and Hills
- ■ Western Corn Belt Plains

Des Moines
Cedar Rapids

1. Dickinson County Nature Center
2. Lost Island Prairie Wetland Nature Center
3. Smith Lake Nature Center
4. Lime Creek Nature Center
5. Heery Woods Nature Center
6. Hartman Reserve Nature Center
7. Upper Mississippi National Wildlife Refuge
8. Bailey's Ford Park Nature Center
9. E.B. Lyons Nature Center
10. Hurstville Interpretive Center
11. Wickiup Hill Outdoor Learning Center
12. Indian Creek Nature Center
13. University of Iowa Museum of Natural History
14. Putnam Museum
15. Jefferson County Park Nature Center
16. Mahaska County Conservation Nature Center
17. Neal Smith National Wildlife Refuge
18. Grimes Farm & Conservation Center
19. Annett Nature Center
20. Bear Creek Nature Center
21. Wolfe Nature Center
22. DeSoto National Wildlife Refuge
23. Neal Moeller Environmental Education Center
24. University of Iowa Museum of Natural History
25. Dorothy Pecaut Nature Center

Most illustrations show the adult male in breeding coloration. Colors and markings may be duller or absent during different seasons. The measurements denote the length of species from nose/bill to tail tip. Butterfly measurements denote wingspan. Illustrations are not to scale.

Waterford Press produces reference guides that introduce novices to nature, science, travel and languages. Product information and hundreds of educational games are featured on the website:
www.waterfordpress.com

Text and illustrations copyright © 2012, 2014 by Waterford Press Inc. All rights reserved. Cover images copyright © iStock Photo. Ecoregion map © The National Atlas of the

To order, call 800-434-2555.
For permissions, or to share comments, e-mail editor@waterfordpress.com. For information custom-published products, call 800-434-2 or e-mail info@waterfordpress.com.

978-1-58355-691-7 $7.95 U.S.
50795
ISBN
9 781583 556917
UPC
8 84682 01006 5
142114

A POCKET NATURALIST® GUIDE

IOWA WILDLIFE

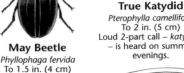

A Folding Pocket Guide to Familiar Animals

IOWA WILDLIFE – A Folding Pocket Guide to Familiar Animals

Kavanagh/Leung

INSECTS & INVERTEBRATES

Nine-spotted Lady Beetle
Coccinella novemnotata
To .25 in. (.6 cm)

May Beetle
Phyllophaga fervida
To 1.5 in. (4 cm)
Often seen flying around porch lights on summer nights.

True Katydid
Pterophylla camellifolia
To 2 in. (5 cm)
Loud 2-part call – katy-DID – is heard on summer evenings.

Deer Fly
Chrysops spp.
To 0.6 in. (1.5 cm)
Females feed on the blood of mammals and deliver a painful bite.

Paper Wasp
Polistes spp.
To 1 in. (3 cm)
Told by slender profile and dark, pale-banded abdomen. Builds papery hanging nests. Can sting repeatedly.

Green Lacewings
Family Chrysopidae
To .75 in. (2 cm)
Clear wings have green veins.

Yellow Jacket
Vespula pensylvanica
To .63 in. (1.6 cm)
Aggressive picnic pest can sting repeatedly.

Honey Bee
Apis mellifera
To .75 in. (2 cm)
Slender bee has pollen baskets on its rear legs. Can only sting once.

Wolf Spider
Family Lycosidae
To 1.5 in. (4 cm)
Has 8 eyes arranged in 3 rows. Most do not weave webs but catch prey by pouncing on it.

Cicada
Tibicen spp.
To 1.5 in. (4 cm)
Song is a sudden loud whine or buzz, maintained steadily before dying away.

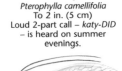

Dog Tick
Dermacentor variabilis
To .25 in. (.6 cm)
Feeds on blood. Can transmit diseases.

Field Cricket
Gryllus pennsylvanicus
To 1 in. (3 cm)
Song is a series of three chirps.

Green Darner
Anax junius
To 3 in. (8 cm)
Has a bright green thorax and a blue body. Like most dragonflies, it rests with its wings open.

Ebony Jewelwing
Calopteryx maculata
To 1.75 in. (4.5 cm)
Like most damselflies, it rests with its wings held together over its back.

Black-and-yellow Garden Spider
Argiope aurantia
To 1.25 in. (3.2 cm)

BUTTERFLIES

Eastern Tiger Swallowtail
Pterourus glaucus
To 6 in. (15 cm)

Black Swallowtail
Papilio polyxenes
To 3.5 in. (9 cm)

Cabbage White
Artogeia rapae
To 2 in. (5 cm)
One of the most common butterflies.

Buckeye
Junonia coenia
To 2.5 in. (6 cm)

Spring Azure
Celastrina ladon
To 1.3 in. (3.6 cm)
One of the earliest spring butterflies.

Eastern Tailed Blue
Everes comyntas
To 1 in. (3 cm)
Note orange spots above thread-like hindwing tails.

Mourning Cloak
Nymphalis antiopa
To 3.5 in. (9 cm)
Emerges during the first spring thaw.

Monarch
Danaus plexippus
To 4 in. (10 cm)

Regal Fritillary
Speyeria idalia
To 3.75 in. (9.2 cm)

Viceroy
Basilarchia archippus
To 3 in. (8 cm)
Told from similar monarch by its smaller size and the thin, black band on its hindwings.

Red-spotted Purple
Basilarchia astyanax
To 3 in. (8 cm)

Question Mark
Polygonia interrogationis
To 2.5 in. (6 cm)
Note ragged wing margins. Silvery mark on underwings resembles a question mark or semi-colon.

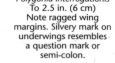

Red Admiral
Vanessa atalanta
To 2.5 in. (6 cm)

American Snout
Libytheana carinenta
To 2 in. (5 cm)
'Snout' is formed from projecting mouth parts which enclose its coiled 'nose'.

Common Checkered Skipper
Pyrgus communis
To 1.25 in. (3.2 cm)

FISHES

Rainbow Trout
Oncorhynchus mykiss To 44 in. (1.1 m)
Note reddish side stripe.

Brook Trout
Salvelinus fontinalis To 28 in. (70 cm)
Reddish side spots have blue halos.

Largemouth Bass
Micropterus salmoides To 40 in. (1 m)
Note prominent side spots. Jaw joint extends past eye.

White Bass
Morone chrysops To 18 in. (45 cm)
Silvery fish has 4-7 dark side stripes.

Bluegill
Lepomis macrochirus
To 16 in. (40 cm)

Crappie
Pomoxis spp. To 16 in. (40 cm)
Note humped back.

Pumpkinseed
Lepomis gibbosus To 16 in. (40 cm)
Green-orange fish has red-black spot on ear flap.

Channel Catfish
Ictalurus punctatus To 4 ft. (1.2 m)
Note adipose fin, black-spotted sides and rounded anal fin.
Iowa's state fish.

Flathead Catfish
Pylodictis olivaris To 5 ft. (1.5 m)
Head is long and flat.

Northern Pike
Esox lucius To 53 in. (1.4 m)
Note large head and posterior dorsal fin.

Walleye
Sander vitreus To 40 in. (1 m)
Note white spot on lower lobe of tail.

Paddlefish
Polyodon spathula To 7 ft. (2.1 m)
Has a long, paddle-shaped snout.

Yellow Perch
Perca flavescens To 16 in. (40 cm)

Common Carp
Cyprinus carpio To 30 in. (75 cm)
Introduced species has an arched back and mouth 'whiskers'.

REPTILES & AMPHIBIANS

Tiger Salamander
Ambystoma tigrinum
To 13 in. (33 cm)
Pattern of yellowish and dark blotches is variable.

Gray Treefrog
Hyla versicolor
To 2.5 in. (6 cm)
Call is a strong, resonating trill.

Northern Leopard Frog
Rana pipiens
To 4 in. (10 cm)
Brown-to-green frog has dark spots on its back. Call is a rattling snore with grunts and moans.

Great Plains Toad
Bufo cognatus
To 4 in. (10 cm)
Call is a metallic trill.

Bullfrog
Lithobates catesbeiana
To 8 in. (20 cm)
Call is a deep-pitched – jug-o-rum.

Chorus Frog
Pseudacris triseriata
To 1.5 in. (4 cm)
Note dark stripes on back. Call sounds like a thumbnail running over the teeth of a comb.

Timber Rattlesnake
Crotalus horridus To 6 ft. (1.8 m)
Note black tail. Venomous.

Eastern Fox Snake
Elaphe vulpina
To 6 ft. (1.8 m)

Common Garter Snake
Thamnophis sirtalis To 4 ft. (1.2 m)
Brownish snake has yellowish back stripe.

Milk Snake
Lampropeltis triangulum
To 7 ft. (2.1 m)

Midland Brown Snake
Storeria dekayi
To 20 in. (50 cm)
Has 2 rows of dark spots down its back.

Eastern Yellow-bellied Racer
Coluber constrictor flaviventris

Eastern Hognose Snake
Heterodon platyrhinos To 4 ft. (1.2 m)
Thick snake has an upturned snout. Color varies.

Prairie Skink
Eumeces septentrionalis
To 9 in. (23 cm)

Western Painted Turtle
Chrysemys picta
To 10 in. (25 cm)

Snapping Turtle
Chelydra serpentina To 18 in. (45 cm)
Note knobby shell and long tail.

Canada Goose
Branta canadensis
To 45 in. (1.14 m)

Snow Goose
Chen caerulescens
To 31 in. (78 cm)
Very common migrant.

Blue-winged Teal
Anas discors To 16 in. (40 cm)

Wood Duck
Aix sponsa To 20 in. (50 cm)

American Coot
Fulica americana To 16 in. (40 cm)

Mallard
Anas platyrhynchos
To 28 in. (70 cm)

Common Goldeneye
Bucephala clangula
To 20 in. (50 cm)

Killdeer
Charadrius vociferus
To 12 in. (30 cm)
Note two
breast bands.

Double-crested Cormorant
Phalacrocorax auritus
To 3 ft. (90 cm)

Great Blue Heron
Ardea herodias
To 4.5 ft. (1.4 m)

Black Tern
Chlidonias niger
To 10 in. (25 cm)

Ring-billed Gull
Larus delawarensis
To 20 in. (50 cm)
Bill has dark ring.

Ruby-throated Hummingbird
Archilochus colubris
To 3.5 in. (9 cm)

Ring-necked Pheasant
Phasianus colchicus
To 3 ft. (90 cm)

Wild Turkey
Meleagris gallopavo
To 4 ft. (1.2 m)

Northern Bobwhite
Colinus virginianus
To 12 in. (30 cm)

Downy Woodpecker
Picoides pubescens
To 6 in. (15 cm)

Red-headed Woodpecker
Melanerpes erythrocephalus
To 10 in. (25 cm)

Northern Flicker
Colaptes auratus
To 13 in. (33 cm)
Wing and tail
linings are yellow.

Pileated Woodpecker
Dryocopus pileatus
To 17 in. (43 cm)
Note large size.

Mourning Dove
Zenaida macroura
To 13 in. (33 cm)
Call is a mournful –
ooah-woo-woo-woo.

Barred Owl
Strix varia
To 2 ft. (60 cm)
Call is a loud –
who-cooks-for-you?
who-cooks-for-
you-all?

American Kestrel
Falco sparverius
To 12 in. (30 cm)

Bald Eagle
Haliaeetus leucocephalus
To 40 in. (1 m)

Rock Pigeon
Columba livia
To 13 in. (33 cm)

Red-tailed Hawk
Buteo jamaicensis
To 25 in. (63 cm)

Northern Harrier
Circus cyaneus
To 22 in. (55 cm)
Note white rump.

Tufted Titmouse
Baeolophus bicolor
To 6 in. (15 cm)

Loggerhead Shrike
Lanius ludovicianus
To 9 in. (23 cm)

Barn Swallow
Hirundo rustica
To 8 in. (20 cm)
Note deeply forked tail.

Black-capped Chickadee
Poecile atricapillus
To 6 in. (15 cm)
Name-saying call is –
chick-a-dee-dee-dee.

Tree Swallow
Tachycineta bicolor
To 6 in. (15 cm)

House Wren
Troglodytes aedon
To 5 in. (13 cm)

White-breasted Nuthatch
Sitta carolinensis
To 6 in. (15 cm)

American Robin
Turdus migratorius
To 11 in. (28 cm)

Eastern Bluebird
Sialia sialis
To 7 in. (18 cm)

Western Meadowlark
Sturnella neglecta
To 9 in. (23 cm)

Gray Catbird
Dumetella carolinensis
To 9 in. (23 cm)
Repetitive call of variable
sounds is interspersed
with cat-like *mew* notes.

Brown Thrasher
Toxostoma rufum
To 12 in. (30 cm)

European Starling
Sturnus vulgaris
To 8 in. (20 cm)

American Crow
Corvus brachyrhynchos
To 22 in. (55 cm)

Cedar Waxwing
Bombycilla cedrorum
To 7 in. (18 cm)
Red wing marks look
like waxy droplets.

Common Grackle
Quiscalus quiscula
To 14 in. (35 cm)

Yellow-headed Blackbird
*Xanthocephalus
xanthocephalus*
To 11 in. (28 cm)

Red-winged Blackbird
Agelaius phoeniceus
To 9 in. (23 cm)

Blue Jay
Cyanocitta cristata
To 14 in. (35 cm)

Yellow Warbler
Dendroica petechia
To 5 in. (13 cm)

House Sparrow
Passer domesticus
To 6 in. (15 cm)

Pine Siskin
Spinus pinus
To 5 in. (13 cm)

Eastern Towhee
Pipilo erythrophthalmus
To 9 in. (23 cm)
Cheerful song is –
drink-your-tea or drink-tea.

Baltimore Oriole
Icterus galbula
To 8 in. (20 cm)

Bobolink
Dolichonyx oryzivorus
To 8 in. (20 cm)

American Goldfinch
Carduelis tristis
To 5 in. (13 cm)
Iowa's state bird.

Blue Grosbeak
Passerina caerulea
To 8 in. (20 cm)

Rose-breasted Grosbeak
Pheucticus ludovicianus
To 9 in. (23 cm)

Purple Finch
Carpodacus purpureus
To 6 in. (15 cm)

Northern Cardinal
Cardinalis cardinalis
To 9 in. (23 cm)

House Finch
Haemorhous mexicanus
To 6 in. (15 cm)

Dark-eyed Junco
Junco hyemalis
To 7 in. (18 cm)

Virginia Opossum
Didelphis virginiana
To 40 in. (1 m)

Big Brown Bat
Eptesicus fuscus
To 5 in. (13 cm)

Eastern Red Bat
Lasiurus borealis
To 5 in. (13 cm)

Thirteen-lined Ground Squirrel
Spermophilus tridecemlineatus
To 12 in. (30 cm)

House Mouse
Mus musculus
To 8 in. (20 cm)
Introduced pest
has a naked tail.

Deer Mouse
Peromyscus maniculatus
To 8 in. (20 cm)
Distinguished by its white
undersides and hairy tail.

Eastern Gray Squirrel
Sciurus carolinensis
To 20 in. (50 cm)

Fox Squirrel
Sciurus niger
To 28 in. (70 cm)
Note large size.

Eastern Chipmunk
Tamias striatus
To 12 in. (30 cm)
Note white stripes
on side and face.

Woodchuck
Marmota monax
To 32 in. (80 cm)

Norway Rat
Rattus norvegicus
To 18 in. (45 cm)
Brown to gray rodent
has a naked tail.

White-tailed Jackrabbit
Lepus townsendii
To 26 in. (65 cm)
Note large ears
and white tail.

Eastern Cottontail
Sylvilagus floridanus
To 18 in. (45 cm)

Common Muskrat
Ondatra zibethicus
To 2 ft. (60 cm)
Aquatic rodent has
a naked tail that is
flattened on its sides.

American Beaver
Castor canadensis
To 4 ft. (1.2 m)

American Badger
Taxidea taxus
To 35 in. (88 cm)

Common Raccoon
Procyon lotor
To 40 in. (1 m)

Least Weasel
Mustela nivalis
To 8 in. (20 cm)

Northern River Otter
Lontra canadensis
To 52 in. (1.3 m)

Striped Skunk
Mephitis mephitis
To 32 in. (80 cm)

Common Gray Fox
Urocyon cinereoargenteus
To 3.5 ft. (1.1 m)

Red Fox
Vulpes vulpes
To 40 in. (1 m)

Coyote
Canis latrans
To 52 in. (1.3 m)
Note bushy, black-tipped tail.

White-tailed Deer
Odocoileus virginianus
To 7 ft. (2.1 m)
Fluffy tail is white below
and held aloft when
running.

Bobcat
Lynx rufus
To 4 ft. (1.2 m)